Feral

JANET MCADAMS grew up in Alabama and attended the University of Alabama, where she was graduated with a B.A. in English and an M.F.A. in Creative Writing. Her Ph.D. in Comparative Literature from Emory University focused on Native American poetry. Her first book, *The Island of Lost Luggage,* won the Diane Decorah Award for Poetry from the Native Writers Circle of the Americas and was published by the University of Arizona Press in 2000. Praised by reviewers as "closely crafted" and "achingly beautiful," the collection received the American Book Award in 2001. She has been a resident artist at the Hambidge Center, the MacDowell "Colony," the Virginia Center, and Ucross. A certified Integral Yoga teacher, she also teaches creative writing and indigenous literature at Kenyon College, where she is the Robert P. Hubbard Professor of Poetry. A writer of Creek and Scottish ancestry, she is the editor of the Earthworks series of indigenous writing for Salt.

Feral

by JANET MCADAMS

CAMBRIDGE

PUBLISHED BY SALT PUBLISHING
PO Box 937, Great Wilbraham, Cambridge PDO CB1 5JX United Kingdom

First published 2007

Printed and bound in the United Kingdom by Lightning Source

Typeset in Swift 9.5 / 13

ISBN-13: 978 1 84471 295 3 paperback
ISBN-10: 1 84471 295 8 paperback

Salt Publishing Ltd gratefully acknowledges
the financial assistance of Arts Council England

1 3 5 7 9 8 6 4 2

For My Parents
who took us to the forest

Contents

It was not power that you lacked, but wishes.

—Randall Jarrell

At the end of the distinguished doctor's
lecture
a young woman raises her hand:

You have the power
in your hands, you control our lives—
why do you want our pity, too?

—Adrienne Rich

The Collectors

i

Audubon in a Waiting Room

But the birds in the prints are dead, she said.
A dozen birds for the one bird you see.

He raced
against earth
pulling
the body toward it.
The end of flight:
owl or heron
feathers dropping
down, flesh sagging
along the wires that hold it
steady
in the picture.

At the doctor's office she pointed out
glassy eyes in the flat print facing us,
where we thumbed magazines
for shades of lipstick, sex tips, creams
to give our skin a certain youthful glow.

Skin loose on the bones, her hair
a half-gone wisp beneath
the scarf wrapped round
and round like a turban.
At least, I thought,
my body hasn't turned on itself,
won't snuff me out before I'm willing
to lie down and stop kicking.

ii
Dream Written Down in Wolf Hour

Never a wing's scales in miniature,
clinging like dust to fingers:
the monarch's brilliant orange,
a swallowtail's lapis blue or butter yellow.
Shells litter the path of uneven walking:

past stuffed owls, trees so rootless,
you could knock them over with a breath of wind.
One snail, grown enormous, stays beside you,
moving along with his muscular foot.

iii
Catalog

Open it, the bursting door:
elephant's foot,
shrunken head,
Princess Venus,
Lemon Cockle,
the Lightning Whelk,
the Hawk Wing Conch,
stuffed fox listing the way
an old man might lean when they've carved out his organs.

Elephants, they say,
encircle the wounded.
The one injured
by spear or misfired gun.

In the foot's dead hollow, umbrellas rise
like ugly misspent flowers.
Ugly flowers for the cold
English rain and parasols
to keep your fair skin from turning
the color of a woman who scrubs
yellow stains from the armpits of blouses.
Blouses you wear for tea, for visiting
a god tacked up and wounded.

iv
Telegram to Sleeper

Oh you who sleep

still sleep
in the room of finite treasure—

v

Instructions for Snail Collectors

On every other Key collectors took a dozen snails
then torched the hammock after them.
The snails more beautiful than jewels
grew rare as emeralds, as secret places.

Remember never to take
more than your fair share. Use
alcohol instead of formalin, which fades
the tree snail's dark red bands.

Look in hardwood hammocks:
the Pigeon Plum or the Wild Tamarind.
It's not so hard to find, if you know where
the Liguus nests. Check the blue-flowered
Lignumvitae, the tree so strong
settlers named it Ironwood
and saw their axes turn.

vi
Petition

Let your mouth fill with dry wings,
your bed with sharp ends of bone,

a tooth hollowed out
rattling in the canvas glove you pull on for gardening. Let

your feet find the path of broken shells,
bits of ivory, the fingerbones of Sioux children,

the broken skull of Osceola, stolen for a talisman,
teeth without their gold fillings, bits of skin

flaking from lampshades, the cracked binding of a book
fat with the story of a boy and his dog Jack or Blue.

Oh sweet adventure with pirates and map, a trunk
so stuffed with gold it will blind the one

who cracks it open.

vii
Call

They say the prey of an owl never hears death coming.

Only
in the air behind you
a change less than weather,
a voice not asking: Who?

It's late today, only
a slant of sun disappearing
into green gone to black in the darkness.

Who that voice will never ask.
Late she says, *Late,* she says, and checks her watch
thinking of a stew she might make for dinner,
whether the milk is too sour for the morning's porridge.

Offices of Pity

. . . Come on, poor babe,
Some powerful spirit instruct the kites and ravens
To be thy nurses! Wolves and bears, they say,
Casting their savageness aside, have done
Like offices of pity.

THE WINTER'S TALE

St. Sernin, 1798

Child, come out of the forest.
I have
porridge thick with cream
to fill your empty belly.

I have a cambric shirt, fine as lawn
to cover your scratched body.

I have a wooden comb
to pull tangles from your wild fur.

History Lesson

Victor flees to the forest, the white lawn shirt
flares in the wind behind him,
and Louis the Sixteenth's blond head
rolls from the guillotine.

Now rational men run the kingdom.
They storm the Bastille, Victor is running, running,
the tough soles of his feet noiseless
on the leafy floor of the forest.

Madame Guerin

I unwind his story like blue yarn
from a wooden spool. Victor, the lost duckling
the human boy licked and petted
by the Queen of Wolves.

Lost, not taken.
His throat scarred by claw not human hand.

Before the boy learned *cold,*
he sat easily in the chilly cottage.

If he could speak, I know he would whisper
ma mere.

Itard: Today's Lessons

Ecoute:
1. You are separate from trees.?
You are separate from wind.

2. There is safety in closed spaces.

3. Milk in the round blue bowl
is the sweet reward
for speaking.

Victor

There is nothing in my story for you.
Your ears
are too full of language.

In the wild kingdom
I drank the sweet milk of my mother.

In the wild kingdom
I was cradled by the warm body of my mother.

Our treasures were teeth and claws
and the wisdom to turn from your cities.

I am not wild, I am not human.
My body has a language. Its scars say: *Be afraid.*
You are weak. Your skin tears easily.

Oh, what key will unlock
the hidden door to the forest?
There each tree is a cradle and wind
the wet-nurse of my childhood.

Twin, Disappearing

Twin sleep-sleeping in the body,
sullen at never waking. Oh child
beyond toes and fingers,
eyes listing to port and starboard
so small when a mother
bled you to water in the doctor's
makeshift office. Or never bled:
you left lodged in the body

of the twinless twin. The months
she gobbled you cell by cell,
but never quite finished.
In your sister's body the tiny useless
extra womb, a third eye covered
with skin or bone, a clot of yellow fat.
One lash sprouting mid-forehead,
plucked like an ordinary stray hair.

A crust of baby teeth beneath the teeth
that bite into the nightly ear of corn.
Voice curled in the left ear like a snail.
Rim of ear a shadow beneath first neckskin,
then shoulderskin, caught beneath the ribs
the way one eye of a flounder
will travel the long flat country of fish
lost deep and blind in the body a lifetime.

The Fish Girl

There is a song the fish girl is singing
as she scales the slick fish with a quick knife.

Another country is the taste of salt water
in the back of her mouth. Her feet ache on dry land.

A conch to the ear and the wind spirals inward.
Breath, a whistle, a voice calling *Sister,*

remember: when you used to breathe water,
how you could taste
with all the fins and scales of your body.

Remember: the song sung to drown sailors.

Oh give back the silver skin
of transformation.

Keeper or lover, give it back.

To the girl with the fishtail,
the one who learned
to walk on dry land

until the Kingdom of Ocean
was a story for children.

A dream of fish flying
through coral trees,
their blue wings fanned open

over the soft bed where all night
she drowns in the dry air.

What She Will Sing to You

My mother cast into the wave that nudged my birth
and I finned out with a slime-covered flipper

and learned a different kind of love:
this dorsal fin could cut you through like a razor.

You will learn to breathe here after all. Over these joined legs
are two fat breasts and a mouth, soft and open. A tongue to wrap

around the words I might whisper, through water, salt water.
Sailor, you can learn to breathe here. Come down, come

down. I was never human, not your fairy tale. I will teach you more
than breathing. I will make your body ache open with salt pleasure.

The Prisoner of Castle Pilsach

If I could sing to you, I would sing,
Kasper Hauser, in your dark cell so long
you have forgotten language, forgotten

the use of legs and crawl across the stone floor
for this day's black bread and water.
There is never enough.

When the man says *walk*, you walk
into Nuremberg with a note for Mayor Binder:
I want to be a rider the way my father was.

But who was father? Who was mother?
The dark womb of your cell? The unknown
jailer? Two broken wooden horses?

In the museum in Ansbach, I saw the brilliant
blues and greens, the fierce paintings
you brought out of the darkness.

In Ansbach you might be safe to find
your mother, your father, to find
your way back to the day you cut your finger

on the witch's spinning thimble
and slept and woke and never really
woke at all. Later, there are dreams:

the woman with the yellow hat,
the man beside her dressed in black,
a sword, a silver, blue-ribboned medal.

The woman called your name,
she called you *Gottfried.* You wept.
You woke yourself with weeping.

But every great man has a theory.
One says: *No one learns language*
late, that late. He could not

have been sleeping all those years.
One says: *He is the lost prince of Baden.*
One asks: *Were there stories in the quiet basement?*

The tourists come to watch you play
with wooden animals.
To watch the boy who talks to animals.

Excited, he told the cat:
Today I have met your cousin.
He said to the cat: You must be obedient

like the obedient dog I met today.
The lost prince ate bread only. He freed
birds from cages. Kasper Hauser—

tell me how you tired of humans
and tried to find your way back to the castle
where *they* slept, waiting:

the two horses, the tiny wooden dog.
Oh how you tried.
Too late they tore down

a wall in the castle to find
your lily-shaped prison window
and the broken wooden horse

who was your friend. By then
your story was lost forever. By then
you were twice dead.

The Polar Journeys

Trapped in the Ice: The *Jeanette*

They will find us preserved in ice like flies
preserved in amber. The bottled ship, its tiny men
in all the postures of our work. We cling
to the frozen sheet. We measure the depth
of the sea we cannot see. We ask: What use for a ship
when water's gone solid? Two years in the pack,
which of us doesn't dream of walking across
the floes around the ship, of even a two-foot
plot of solid land? Which of us does not dream
of a warm bed, a human body?
Which of us knows his body anymore?
We toss our foolish science out, sextants, theodolites
a dozen metal gadgets. On all the lost barometers,
the needles swing past *foul* to *killing cold*.

Baleen: The Whale Boats

Whalers pick their way north to the 90th parallel.
and blue whales lace the sides
of breathless Victorian wives and daughters.

This second ribcage holds them steady,
beneath dull light squeezed
from the thick yellow fat whales float on.

Like lines of longitude,
the baleen limns the hourglass landscapes
of their waiting bodies.

The whalers catalog the krill
from each whale's stomach, fish out ovaries,
and search the guts for a lump of ambergris
large as a fist or a head.

This is history: that every world grows smaller.

The *Eagle*: Andree and Frankel, 1897

Thirty-three years after your balloon touched down
on the ice island east of Spitsbergen,
a passing ship discovered the end of your story:
a stack of diaries and seventeen rolls of film.
A year the labs worked overtime—
then the images cleared. Time on your hands,
you photographed everything, the damaged *Eagle*,
Frankel, full of pride, over the huge polar bear body.
It's clear you cannot believe your luck.
Curled like an infant in the foreground, that bear
was your death, though you didn't know it as you ate
the raw, tainted meat and curled inside the tent and died.

The National Geographic Book of Polar Explorers

In my *National Geographic Book of Polar Explorers*,
they leave out all the crucial information:
whether it's worse to reach your goal
and turn back and start for home and perish.
Or find yourself trapped in ice a mere three days
after starting.
              In the book, they never say
what flesh might have to do with any of these stories:
the *Jeanette*'s engineer carried a drought of poison
to taint his cells so his companions could never eat him.
The blackening and frozen toes, Peary's, I've heard,
snapped off with his rabbit-skin socks.
Instead they came to us intact, full of spirit.
The men who thought they made the world their home.

Cairns

The first cairn holds the captain's story,
a letter to his wife. The next is stuffed
with animals and birds, the naturalist's
drawings of the world he takes to sleep with him.
In the third cairn, ten bodies to be hauled
the thousand miles to Irkutz. Thawed and embalmed,
they cross Russia by rail and start the watery
voyage home. The continents line up:
a syzygy of history, across the chill distances
of this world. A clumsy statue tops the captain's tomb
at Woodlawn. None of it is worth the grave nearby
stuffed with the bodies of men no one claimed,
these eighty milder winters since their death.

The Children's Map of Antarctica

Who knows how long Andree and Frankel lasted.
Or if they quarreled, as all the men who struck out

for the ice did sooner or later. On the map, the five
emperor penguin eggs are marked in black.

The Adelie penguins dance in clusters on Adelie land.
White streaks mark the vapor trail the huskies left

in the chilly air. At the 85th parallel, Socks, the luckiest
of Shackleton's five ponies, is shown tumbling into a crevasse

with the sledge he hauled across the Antarctic.
He lives there still in a magic underworld,

a Manchurian-pony, penguin, polar bear Atlantis,
where all the creatures breathe ice instead of water.

Reader, I'm making this up, but face it:
the strange world is below us, above us, and beyond.

Snow Blindness

The Manchurian ponies weep in the sharp wind.
The blindness starts with reddened eyes,
then weeping, and grit beneath the clumsy goggles.
You rub your eyes, but nothing changes:
It's clear too late you were mistaken.
The ponies' hooves are heavy in the snow.
Beneath the ice, the lost ones sleep.

Is there a solstice at the pole?
When this cold world turns again
toward summer, what will
their thawed words tell us?
Beneath the ice they sleep,
their frozen words caught in water
like fish who sleep away the winter.

The Polar Journeys

In all my polar journeys, where were you?
I looked for you in the face of a man
who slept with a gun on his night side table.
My blood flowed slow as a glacier.

This world is so unsteady. The floes I camp on
break apart and new ice bends beneath my feet
like rubber.

This world's a mouth that sucks you in.
A mouth so toothed with ice, white waves of it,
sastrugi slice our boots to ribbons.

I'm too far north, I'm out of touch
with everyone I've ever loved. My heart's
a fist of ice beneath the anorak,
this skin of fur I wear against the frozen world.

The Sister of the Swans

The sister roamed the world to find:
her twelve brothers, changed by a father's
thoughtless wish. In the forest cottage
where they lived, they ate from swan-
sized plates and slept in beds too cramped
for their human sister. For years,
they lived like this: between two worlds.
The sister slept on a pallet when she found them.

The sister rode on a net across the ocean,
like a web carried in the beaks of twelve
spiders. She took the spell's vow of silence
before she met the King, who loved her
for her modest ways. He was sure she nodded
the day his huntsmen dragged her
to the castle and he asked her to marry. Six
of the seven years he loved her less and less.

For seven years she worked at night to sew
the twelve nettle shirts that would release
her brothers. She gathered the stinging
nettles from the neglected graves of children.
The King shared no part of this story.
Her modest glances turned to secretive looks
and the Queen Mother whispered: *See how she
steals from your bed late at night.*

Late at night, the King imagined her lovers
one after another. Still, she could not speak.
She moved easily through the air, like her mute swan
brothers, as she gathered the nettles in silence.
The swan brothers saved her from the King's harsh
punishment in the nick of time. Their wings beat out
the flames, their beaks pulled loose the cords that bound her,
as the grieving King looked on in love and hatred.

Of course, the grieving King rejoiced to see
the long spell broken, when the brothers put on
the shirts that transformed them. But there were
so many brothers. The youngest was saved
by a shirt with one sleeve missing. Sickened, the King
averted his glance. His wife's voice was low and rough,
not at all the way he'd imagined. He wondered
at the lullaby she sang the prince, a boy with downy hair.

The swan princes' wild laughter rang out in the castle.
The Queen put her loom away: she was tired of weaving.
Once, the King heard her hiss at the cook. At night,
hands burning with the memory of nettles, the King snoring
uneasily beside her, did she long for the midnight churchyard?
The King longed for the sweet girl he married,
each time he heard the graceful swish of her garments
or felt her elegant white neck between his hands.

The Animal Baths

*To treat her ailing right hand, Clara Schumann was prescribed "animal baths,"
a remedy in which the patient inserted the afflicted hand into the freshly
slaughtered carcass of an animal.*

i

In Leipzig, Herr Wieck is writing his daughter's diary,
while the wunderkind Clara plays the étude again and again.
"Father," he begins and writes her story for her:
each tour, the meeting with Goethe, how carefully

her father taught her: Clara, the delicate girl
with hands so large she could play for hours.
A husband who took her away and wrote and wrote
while she tiptoed around the house afraid to practice.

Owned by father, then husband, then seven hungry mouths,
her right hand aches past salt baths, wooden contraptions,
a fortnight of treatments to play the serenade in Paris.

ii

To Brahms, she writes: I have taken the water treatment.
She writes: If *you* were the father of seven—

By his asylum bed, Schumann propped a picture
not of her, but a pencil drawing
of the seventeen-year old Brahms.
He looked at it and starved.
The doctors said: You must not visit.

iii

Break open the body of sow, sweet young calf, or goat
in his shaggy coat. Let the skin yield to bear
this salt potion, the hot flush of life into ulna,
radius, one stiff finger, then another.

The smell of bowels loosening while the adagio
plays ear to ear.

When the concertmaster raises his bow, she will touch
her blood-marked fingers to the ivory keys

whether her hand is healed by wishing
or by the blue heart of an animal beating,
in compound time against her aching fingers.

Letter from the Crimea

Florence to Parthe Nightingale

I had a dream, Parthe, where one soldier's
body grew enormous beneath my hands.
They've grown so calloused these twelve days

at Scutari. Six of the women left the first day.
It wasn't blood or fever that drove them
from us and those who stayed,

they learned to cut and stitch, to stand
for thirty hours. Sister, don't envy me!
I know we will never love each other.

If I've had a sister, it was Mary.
If we could choose our dreams,
I would be with her, walking arm in arm

in the Rue de Bac, or side by side
in her salon. You never liked her.
In my dream, the body grew and grew—

I could not help but enter it, enter that house
of flesh and humid air. The lamp before me
flickered out, but one light burned

the long dull morning 'til I woke. I've seen more
of men's bodies than you could imagine.
The husband I don't envy, the one who wanted me—

What does he long for when he rubs his face
against the bone buttons of your chemise?
I know what happens. Soldiers talk.

In listless dreams they talk and dream themselves
back into perfect bodies. They long for more
than the absence of pain or cold or fear of death,

of death alone in a foreign country.
You could have gone with me,
but you would not *be* me. Across my bedroom,

light cuts sharp as a saber. The nights I sleep,
I sleep alone. Sickness is the lover
whose heat I lean into. Envy me then, Sister.

The Green Children

Brought as curiosities to the house of a certain knight, Suffolk, 1150

Eyewitness

In Suffolk, the light was so bright, the air so fierce,
they lay down senseless.
They lay down beside the wolf-pit
until, fresh from fields slouched with haystacks,
reapers found them.

Their skin grew light on a diet of whey and barley,
the dense brown peasant bread, linnets snared
on the limed branches of ash.
The green girl became like everyone else, baptized
and married. But her brother grew sick with longing.

When his jewel-green skin faded white
as a fish's underbelly, the green boy died
on a white English day.

Storyteller

It is said: When captured, they wept bitterly.
It is said: They refused food, breaking open
only the pods of fresh peas.

When she learned to speak English,
the green girl told them everything
they wanted to hear:
her land was a Christian country
though locked in twilight,
pulled by the sound of a bell
sister and brother entered a long cave
in the land they called St. Martin's
and found themselves in England,
the gate home closed forever.

Most of the story is lost to history:
whether they were the color of holly or citrine,
if their hair shone like emeralds or lay
dull as jade along their scalps.

The Sister

The English had never heard
of the twilight St. Martin's.
The green girl said she was eager
to take up the work of the knight's demesne:
To soak and comb the flax
until her fingers bled.
To weave a linen slip to wear beneath
the coarse russet wool of the dress they gave her.
To rise in the dark and lay her head
against a wall of cow
and squeeze until the last drop
of yellow milk was wrung
from its pink nipples.

The nights she whispered
over her brother's green grave:
In this bright country, grass grows in blades.
Each field is a crowd of sharp edges.

They taught me blue: *the sky where song birds*
mob the fierce brown hawks that steal their young.

They taught me red: *the color of mouths crying open.*

The One Who Died

But the one who died instead of speaking,
never told them:

In our soft country we never knew we were green.
The world was moss, water cool as the depths
of any well you might drink from. Our mother's hair
wafted like the fronds of ferns that grow
thick as fingers along the river. Our father's voice
was a low hum, sweet as bees' wings in the dusk
of green meadows.

Oh never go there. Let them live, my kinsmen
in the twilight country. Not this
hard light. Glare and shadow.
We never needed this journey.

The Orphan Train

Based on the practice of "placing out" children to farm communities in the Western United States, 1853–1929

Violet says she cannot sleep for fear of wolves
and savages, but her head nods into my lap
and we doze across the territories.

Sister Michaela bought bread and yellow apples
from a woman whose shawl was the color
of peaches. I have not yet seen peaches.

She held her fat daughter tight by one hand.
But when her mother turned toward the train
to call out, *Botanos! Pan dulce!*

I saw the girl dance a moment on tiptoe.
In the Hotel Morenci, we sleep four to a bed.
I dream the house they took me from,

the boy with black eyes who teased and teased,
until I cried and asked for Sister. He gave me this,
the doll of red and yellow cloth I am holding.

Sister says Father Mandin should not have given us
to a Mexican family, though they are good Catholics.
She is sure the white ladies will take us,

so every evening, I tie Violet's straight
brown hair into sausage curls.
We weren't unhappy at the school in Boston.

We had oatmeal every morning, and sometimes the milk
was thick and blue with cream. I had two dresses,
a brown domestic trimmed with scarlet ribbon

and the white French linen I am wearing, today,
for Sunday service. I pressed it myself, mixing
the cake of sweet starch into water

and sprinkling, sprinkling until the steam
clouded my eyes and they ran with tears.
When we left, Mary Margaret cried

and tried to climb into the wagon with us.
We begged Sister though we knew no family
would take a girl who could not work.

The Sunday she came to us, our white dresses
surrounded her and she cried out, *Engelskinder!*
Soon we taught her how to count to five on her fingers,

and the words, children, angel, and home.
The train became our home. We slept in motion.
We did not know then what childhood was.

Buffalo in Six Directions

Riddle

the long day   left to languish
flesh forgotten   hide hacked

I hurtled   hard-hooved
out of this century

Recipe

Rub the hide with brain to soften it.
Pack the stomach with cherries and roast
over a slow fire or stew
with cherry juice, spices
to mask the wildness
but that wild taste
lingers on the tongue the way
we thought we saw them
one hungry winter
so many winters
after they disappeared.

Measures

Lewis & Clark: "200 miles of buffalo"

One kill = a week of meat

"the world"—he wrote—"looked like one robe"

Letter

My Dearest One,
When the train stopped dead from hard winter
they came out of nowhere, the herd
looking for shelter
pushing against the train
though we shouted, rang bells,
and shot into them.

Nothing would stop them,
so we held fast and waited.
Some froze standing, some
curled together.
One of the soldiers hacked off a head for a trophy,
so large, he could barely wrestle it onto the train,
larger than our Emily when I left Boston last summer.

If you saw such fur, you could not imagine a cold
bitter enough to pierce it.
I was grateful for the divine cold
but couldn't help but wonder
why has He sent us into this country
so filled with monsters and savages.

Journal

Tuesday 17th. Shot at three bulls but missed all.

Wednesday 18th. Wrote a letter to my beloved Agatha.

Thursday 19th. Killed two young bulls today though the last
would not go down. Pumped his skin
so full of lead. We pickled the meat in the Great Salt Lake.

Friday 20th. Return to England on the morrow. A successful
journey:
79 bears, and 180 buffalo hides.
Enough hides for a dozen lifetimes!

Riddle

We hurtled   hard-hooved
thundered down   dusty plains

like stalks of   lupine rising
We ran past   bones piled

into towers   beautiful bonfires
left to languish   the long day

we disappeared.

Interview with the Reader

1. She gave you a list. What were the first three questions?

2. What windows did you cover? What doors were boarded up against the bitter winter?

3. Did a phoebe call out *fee-bee*? Did the mockingbird say your name?

4. Was it only a flesh wound? Did anyone suffer?

5. What was the song that the heart learned to whistle? Did the bell have a tongue? What did you know about silence, before you fell through the clear sky air?

6. And what was left in the knapsack, in the abandoned basket at the lakeshore? What was left after summer burned like a clear yellow thread into autumn?

1. Woods to go to, the fish-shaped leaves of lilies,
   well water with its arc of rust.

2. There were no windows. Every door hung open.

3. I heard a name but it was not my name.
   I heard a name but it was only an echo.

4. Are there other kinds of wounds? I am not tired of happiness.

5. Only the lub-dub of the body's river, pushing and pulling,
   the daily wave of flotsam and jetsam. I knew
   a different kind of quiet.

6. The ribs of an umbrella that no longer closes.
   A gold ring from a woman's finger.
   This book, which you've opened,
   when your ear yearns toward another story.

The Daughter of No One

A gold crown lifted and left in the forest.
A black dog with a secret.
Reeds braided into a basket filled with tobacco leaves. Like
postcards from a voyage to the New World.
Hard water clogging tap, drain, the shower where you will never
get clean.
The tobacco leaves lie down like a carpet.
In the jungle's green yellow: animals cackle and hoot, stealing
the girl child.
She learns to tear meat with her sharp baby teeth.

～

The Daughter of No One
In the left-hand doorway
touches a finger to her lips
in warning.
Her face is a dried apple of sorrow.
Not the apples the terror trees
tossed at us, Scarecrow.
Here is a box of parts for the asking:
wooden whistle,
heart that looks like velvet
but is red fur, matted, a smell of flesh rising.

～

If you want this story, you must bargain me down.

～

the way
a suitcase, stored for months,
will shift and sigh without warning.

~

Will shift and sigh over the hard bargain
the delicate Ah—
Half a cough, an *ahem* of pleasure.
Spelled out like an alphabet
A calendar in x's and y's.
Here are the rules for dreaming:
a schedule for the day after sleeping.

~

Clap of thunder, yellow stream of
dust, rough oval of sweat
on a man's gray shirt.
Yellow rose on the bank.
on the bank of the creek thick with blood.
Hide, carcass,
dragged out the cellar door.
I had flesh beneath my fingernails. I had
sinew caught between my teeth.

~

Flat, the world pressed out of breath. Breathing:
O, sigh me back to sorrow
I am so sick of tomorrow.
Bring me a feather, a leaf, a bowl
filled with jelly.
Whistle, purse, castigate, loll. O, my helpless one,
your life, your silly life. I am the milly-
molly of your strongest desire, your
Personal Pinocchio.

~

Red ribbon on a girl's tender neck.
Not cloth, but blood. O let
the head not topple, let
the red be anything but.
Seven golden curls: give one to each brother.
Come under
the gathering — *I am sick*
of my bag of tricks—
clouds. Soft as velvet
the shrinking map of discovery
where white horses
of waves
ride the sea down to sand.

Dreaming, the Book of

i

The one about horses, wild with terror
running past, running over
anklebone, the long muscle of thigh,
the *C C C*
of hoofmark on hip,
on ribcage, on scapula.

The dream where dancers reached for you
as they circled by.

The ones about flying.
The one dream about starving.

The dream where water calls to water
tugging the body toward
lake river ocean
the salt water that will scrub
a wound from its history.
The dream where skin
in love with water
will crease and fold to drink in more,
each cell opening
its dry, dry throat.

ii
You could have let
the crescent moon hook you into flight.
Or the white flower
sing you to sleep.
Every leaf edge, every flower.
Light cutting the green lawn in two at twilight.
The pitch black corner at the back of the yard.
Sleep cut by stories of your making.
Sullen blue midnight or the bleached gray wolf hour—waking.
The bed with its sheets pulling away from the mattress.
The collie curled
in an *O* at your feet.
The sky lit by the town in the distance.
The dream you wrote in a letter.
The one you saved in a jar.
The dream where they reached for you
but you pulled back saying
not me not
this time.
The landscape of longing and hiding.
The landscape of longing.
The portrait of running, of turning away,
of turning. Painted all night
sleeping or dreaming.
Sleeping and waking.

Ghazal of Body

Teach me the story of the sleepless body.
Even the past is ugly, living as it does in the thick cells of my body.

I was lonely, all the long winter. Skin
the poorest fence between the cold world and my body.

The fisherman with his sharp hook, his taut line, a rod he is proud of.
Come to shore, I call, I have a handful of bread that might be your body.

Lace, you breathed against the window, and the ice let go,
ran down the glass into the house's quiet body.

She said: *When I gave him up, when I gave back the baby,*
there was an empty space in front of my body.

No writ, no photograph, no stone with rules. Only memory,
running like a current of blood, through the creek of my body.

One Day the Girl

One day the girl
took the tube
from her throat
and went out walking,
felt the ground beneath
her puckered, tender feet.
A crow asked her name
and a grey fox
rubbed against her legs
the way a cat rubs
against a guest
expecting nothing.
All of the animals
grew tired of weeping

for her, the girl

with the aching throat.
They cried to let
their salt tears
mend the years
of her wound,
raw flesh from the tube
that said she
couldn't be trusted.

They grew tired long
before she could whisper:
Fox, come back
with a story at the corner of your mouth.
Not the story of a white room
with a window
but of this place
green so deep
it turns to black in the shadow.

Wind, make the sound of
sleeping in the trees.
Make a sound like a sigh,
this sound I make
as I learn not to whisper.

Body, catch fire
until the pale light of sorrow
heads out to sea,
leaves this body
its hills and furrows
leaves this land
its salt veins
its bone and sinew.

The Way the World Comes Back

When did you notice it was no longer winter?
Skin sloughing away after the dry cold?
Or the moment you shed
the heavy coat you wear against the world?

This paring down is no small matter.
The urge to crack and cast away
the shell the body forged from years of grief.
The way the knife can't help but slip
and so much of the work must be done at twilight.

But what if the world came back?
Even in miniature or scarred.
Lush green or bruised yellow.
Wind strong enough to lift feather or leaf,
unravel the long scarf from your throat,

to sweep the dust from stone,
uncover bone or story.
What if your stone heart turned to salt?
What if it turned to water
and roared through your body like an ocean?

Girl in Phone Booth

She thinks: I remember my father
over there waving, before I left before

my nose started bleeding. The acacias
bloomed although it was winter.

The town crier gobbled the news:
3 soldiers with a magic

recipe: pocket of onions,
some salt, a bowl of milk.

It's easy to make soup
with a trick

easy to see stars
if you look at them sideways.

Daughter leaning against the glass wall
your dropped coin rolls and

rolls, into the gutter, then
the hands of a boy caught

in the jaws of an alligator, the
underground monster

surfing the city's canals.
Only a wish, a magic

gold ring could rescue
the lost coin, only the father's voice

answering at the other end.

Moths

"Coloured after Nature," in *Captain Brown's Book
of Butterflies and Moths*, the glossy wings of the Proserpina
shift from black to dull midnight blue the way they do

in Nature. The artist had to imagine the moth intact, unpinned,
from the nearly perfect specimen Captain Brown kept between
the Twin-Striped Tabby and the Clear-Winged Humming Sphinx.

Captain Brown's collection was the marvel of London.
A room stacked with shallow drawers, where the moths might
have been sleeping, row upon row: the Tiger, the ashen gray

Peppered Moth, the rare, magnificent Emperor, most striking of all:
the Luna, a ghostly face shining from pale green wings. No one
was allowed to touch.

～

All night in the borrowed studio
the endangered Luna beat with fury
against the tall window.
I couldn't write for watching it.
I couldn't sleep for listening.

I shut off every light
but still it battered.

Light or the memory of light,
each the same sweet poison.
The summer I first began to know you.
The summer I lost track
of the boundaries
of my body.

～

The morning I woke
with a vein pulsing on, off and on,
all along the right side of my face,
half the world a shadow of pain.

No vision like Hildegaard's.
No aura, flashing lights, clear trigger:
like the man who saw snow falling
and lay down to a three-day migraine.
Only: the pent-up currents of a body curled into itself.

 ∼

The pent-up currents the doctor let loose
needle by needle.

Now, I thought,
he will pin me back together again.

He said:
Beautiful and needled me down,
point by point: wrist, ankle, sternum,
the soft flesh between forefinger and thumb.

He said: *You
are a very beautiful woman* and touched my breasts
with his two hands.

 ∼

In the difficult landscape of telling,
they ask: Did you pay?
the men imagine the struggle,
they turn from the damage.

The women say, What did he *say?*
and tell me, *When I was twelve* . . .
Or *Once my mother's doctor* . . .
Or *His tongue in my mouth, His hands
there or there* . . .

          ~

Did I imagine the doctor's hand shaking
when he pushed in the last needle,
the needle straight through the vein of it?

Beneath my eye, blood blossomed
dull violet.
A scarlet letter. *A shiner!*
someone said,
laughing clear past the face of my pain.

          ~

In 1782, English citizens gather in their churches
to pray for relief from the ravenous brown tail moth.
It came in hordes and stripped trees bare of leaves.

They prayed not for leaves but that the moth's arrival
was *odd circumstance, and not God's judgment.*
But these were the prayers of the vulgar, the Captain reports,

for the moths afforded a seasonable admonition: *How easy
the comforts,* Captain Brown is philosophical, *nay even
the existence of man, assailed by a creature so insignificant.*

          ~

Pinned against velvet.
Soothed by laudanum.
They forget about dying. Every
one
is a curiosity.

~

I would tell you a different story if I could.
But every one of us is the girl with the dirty uncle.
Against our skin is every pinch and grope.
Before our eyes, photos of women chained
and cut, girls bent
to impossible positions.

What pain we would suffer over
and over. Over
doctors who pierce
the bodies we think they can mend.

Where is the room apart?
Where is the place we will lie down?
Your words get lost
in the louder music of whistles and calls

All your life, in pity for your innocence,
women who loved you told you
only what you could bear to hear.
What I hear is relentless and uneven.
I cannot sleep for listening.

The Children of Animals

It was the beginnings they were sure about:
Itard, the Reverend Singh, Madame Guerin
who knew the boy was human when she touched him.
She loved her feral child until he died at forty.
In Midnapore, though, Singh's first thought was this:
to keep the wolf girls' secret, Amala and Kamala,
found in an ant mound in 1920, for fear they'd
never marry. They never knew their ancestors:
Victor, of course, the Irish Sheep Boy, even
Clever Hans, tapping out his master's answers.
Itard was younger then than I am now, and eager
for his *tabula rasa*, the child captured at St. Sernin,
a slate to chalk in all the science of his time.

Itard tried, I'll give him that, to transform Victor
from feral to human. *I wanted to extend,* he writes,
his physical and social needs. Victor learned, in time,
to feel the cold, to drink from bowls. He learned
Itard's peculiar sense of justice, locked in a closet
one sunny afternoon. He never knew Itard
was testing him, that he rejoiced at Victor's
outraged tears. Yes, Victor cried sometimes
unlike Amala, who wept that once, at fourteen
when her sister died. They were Singh's only
wild children, but not his only captives. He caught
a few from every tribe in the dense Indian jungle
and sent them home filled with Christian ways.

Could it have been a trick to fool the earnest Singh?
He must have gasped to see the mother wolf,
the cubs and her two human charges. And did they
kill the wolves? I've always wondered. The sisters'
palms were thick with skin. On hands and feet, they ran
like A-frames through the compound—I've seen
the blurry photographs. They say they ate raw meat
and milk and neither of them ever married.
The sisters lived a hundred years past Victor,
the feral boy of Aveyron, the one who learned
to feel the cold, and graduated Itard's desperate
training. He passed his later years at Chez Guerin—

the cottage in the Rue du Bac around the block
from Victor Hugo, who translated him into Quasimodo.
It was the later years that gave the doctor problems.
He didn't visit. And Reverend Singh, how pleased
was he the day Amala finally walked upright?
She knew the name of every baby in the compound
though not much more. And yet I think she knew
she never lived by words. Like Victor,
the boy who loved the vowel O, who ran away,
not once but three times, pulled back—who can know?—
by milk or love or warmth or words.

Wing

Hawk, I would like to unimagine your death,
whether you wrenched yourself
free of the barbed wire

and lingered, gimp-bird, stunned
to find you could not fly or navigate.
Phantom wing pushing the air
like a pillow clouding you into sleep
forever.

Or if coyotes took you down.
Or men with metal objects.

I have nine feathers from your wing—
the side turned toward the sun

is glossy black, the underside—
cream cut across with stripes of brown.
Fanned out across the desk where I try
to write you down

beside an apple withering
like a heart awaiting a new
host body.
Oh, how beautiful

the red hair of the woman who came
to clip feather from bone, to wash
each one like a breakfast dish rimmed with egg
or a scum of milk. To dry the wispy barbs tender as

a child's brown curls. Who scraped

the tip of red flesh, the lost flesh
of your lost wing. The bone like a chicken wing
sucked dry at a picnic. Oh, had I

found you sooner, you would have clawed me raw,
my human hands, my human
face. You would never have endured saving.

A Natural History of Hands

Anna Mae Pictou Aquash

i
Five days in the desert not dying
but dead and no one asking.

Two hands in a box
still as ashes, not crawling.

Still as ashes, not crawling
like spiders.

No box breaking open
postal worker screaming:
Look, look what's in this box!—

The Addams Family: two friends for Thing.

A ring stand × 2.

Five fingers gilded
for Cocteau's *Beauty and the Beast*.
How they clutch Beauty's velvet mantel
when she hangs it up.

Not velvet, but denim and torn cotton.
Not Beauty: An Indian woman left for dead in the desert.

In this story, hands never scuttled like spiders
across the floor of the morgue where they cut her up.

Reader: Nothing crawled across your face late at night.
Nothing.

ii
Hands, no escape for you either
however you long
for the mother body
the dead weight of past lives
your own paragraph in a book
written years after.
Did her mother think, pushing her out
in a flood of blood and mucous—
Did she think: These hands
will enter history?

What stories did the doctor find written on
tendon, muscle, bone?
One finger pointing, three scratching
a mosquito bite behind the knee.
Nails bitten, hair twined round and round
a single index finger.
Dough kneaded, a shirt mended,
each fist made in fear or anger,
every wave to say goodbye.

Sanctuary

Too easy to say
you were the spirit of kingfisher
the day we carried
your heavy bag of ashes
through the dense pine forest
of the preserve.
At the pond, we watched you scatter.
I still can't believe
what the body comes down to.

Your daughter told me how you
stayed with her, and stayed
through the difficult days after.
When you went away,
she left the house
of the father who touched her
when he shouldn't have touched her.
Three nights she wept
in the unheated attic
of your empty house.

This is no love poem to dying.
Everyone dies.
Every family learns
the intricate language of cancer.
Shunt or *chemo*—words easy as
paper or *mayonnaise*
when the mouth longs to say
Next year or *When we,*
the way it longs for salt,
the way it longs for water.

Too easy to say: that bird, your passing.
But I know how, in the last days,
you sorrowed for the life
your frail daughter
would lead without you.
At the bird sanctuary
we saw only the one bird, laughing,
its blue wings open
over the pond
where your ashes floated.
Kingfisher,
the bird that can slip into water—
invisible after the water closes over.

Ghost Ranch

Light picks this landscape down to bone.
It's Boxing Day. The orange jumpsuits
six miles back pick trash while they do time.
The guards in their blue suits are white.
Someone has cut the Indian prisoners' hair.

The mesa's one short hard haul straight up.
Gray feather in the crack I work my fingers
into and tug and work them out again.
Then flat on top and land for miles and miles—
so much land. You find a pile of bones

and hold the pelvis up to frame a ragged disc
of sky. Not the real sky, I thought that day,
but blue enough to tell this story. You say
the feather's from a dove and spot an eagle
circling high across the canyon, but I am not

so sure. We touch and circle and touch and circle
until we only circle: cloth against cloth, skin
not quite meeting, the way fences touch at the corners
of nations. Last night you slept so quietly,
I put a hand to your back to make sure

you were breathing, the other over your shoulder
and flat against the skin between breast
and solar plexus because breath may not be
a sure enough measure. We hover
over the animal that carved itself

this place to rest, past molecule, atom,
the stinging energy that drums the universe
into being. Don't say you never felt it.
Even the stone was pulsing. Take my hand
if you can bear it, but let the other story go.

Earth My Body Is Trying to Remember

i

Crows are all black angles.
One comes down from the trees,
calls to us
in the shape of a yellow dog

running, running: its call
sharp as a bird with a secret.
We huddle together, we hurry, we wish
the moon were up.

By morning, the light so fierce
we flatten beneath it. Oil leaks
from our bodies, sacks dry as raisins.
I wrap a shawl around my face.
I hang the bed sheets up to dry

and clothes on the line
empty of the bodies that shaped them.
They flap in the long sleeve of wind.
All the children go crazy in the wind.

ii

We followed the trail through the forest,
strangled by the thick air of the ravine.

Looking for traces, how we circled and
circled back. Ashamed of our thirst.

That train all night rails clicking.
You slept and woke and woke

and slept an hour past exhaustion.
Not the lights flashing

could've stirred your sleep.
Not whistle, loud argument

from the dining car, or the old woman
whose carpet bag bumped your sleeping shoulder.

I kept watch over the passing houses
a row of yellow lights

then a pocket of darkness
green

as the inside of a well in September.
The girl who fell down it.

The gold ring
misplaced for generations.

iii

Scattered in the green field
a herd of cattle without flesh or hide.

I found a bone
thick as my wrist
and one spindly as a finger
reaching through a clump of grass.
A rib cage porous and listing
to one side like a small boat
swamped in a storm:
the sister screaming over the wind—

The only fish our only dinner.
Its long body slit and flattened
a butterfly of flesh
sizzling in the skillet's old grease.
Every meal in this house
seasoned with salt and lard
year after year
thickening on the surface.

iv

The bone rustlers ride by.
Their white breath
a cloud in the air after horses.

A tree leans down to say:
You must not follow.

I flew over the city
and saw two girls argue
over a necklace of white beads.
I heard a dog whine
but it was only a rusty hinge,
a door pulled open
a runaway surprised
from his bed of hay
knapsack left in flight
in fright my father
brought it into the kitchen light
my mother's face grew tight
at the contents: a picture torn
from the newspaper, a knot
of string, knife blade dull
and missing its handle.

I saw a doorway that looked
like the absence of a boat.
I saw a streetlight grow leaves.
I saw melted skin turn to bark
veins stretched out like black pipe
twisting as blood pumped

and pumped through
to the cellar.

I looked down a fissure where the street
had cracked
open—into dust and red flesh.

v

Imagine a flight that begins in water.

On the ocean, too still or storming.
The sun calls itself wind and either way
it's in your eyes.

The fisherman with his sharp hook—
Come to shore, I call, I have a handful of bread for your dinner.
If he hears, my voice
does not turn his body.
This green water is thick enough to lie down on.

Oh sky full of water
come down to land and let us swim over.

vi

Water, let go.
I would crawl from here onto shore.

Salt, scrub wounds from flesh.
Let these lost bones settle.

Leaves, sing me down.
I am sick of floating.

Ice, come back to water
or let me sleep
on your white bed of winter.

Earth, my body
is trying to remember.

vii

Hard luck turned the river brown
and a dog with a broken throat
sang when he wanted to be barking.

All of the animals are still in their cages.
All of the pictures snapped into vinyl albums.
A factory blows smoke over the choking town.

I am claw waiting to sink into the tender flesh of your throat.
I am pelt, glass eyeball, thinning red flesh.
A tire floating down the river, once burning.

viii

The road from the village wound up and up
and we huddled in our makeshift cabin.
A lantern burned against stories
from the past that knocked and knocked
and knocked again when we did not answer.

One night a light in the woods moved closer and closer
then vanished. The white fields murdered summer.

ix

We were born but born too young to remember.

The land they took us from, the mothers' milk dried up,
every womb a dried-up
crackle of flesh. Earth my body
is trying to remember.

Child-That-Was, don't try to remember, but lean back
into this place outside history.
Lean into the bright color climbing the stone wall
as if violet against grainy white or pale blue crocuses
were the end of the story.

Violet or amber, the color, the flower,
the jewel most rare
when it traps an insect for eternity.
They chipped away at us,
hammered us out like gold.

A river flowed by slow as mercury.

In the night of black jade, we
were more than meat, more
than a handful of carbon.

We were cell and stone and field, the sky:
Stars pulled down from their wandering.

Several of the poems in this volume retell or refer to stories about feral children. **Offices of Pity** was inspired by Truffaut's film *L'Enfant Sauvage*; much of the information in the poem comes from J.M. Itard's journals about "training" Victor, the Wild Boy of Averyron. **Children of Animals** focuses on the so-called Wolf Girls of India. The information in my poem comes from the Reverend Singh's own account in *Wolf-Children and Feral Men*. While there are many accounts of the odd story of Kasper Hauser (**The Prisoner of Castle Pilsach**), Jeffrey Masson's thorough *Kasper Hauser* is a book notable for its compassionate treatment of Hauser's short life. Douglas Candland's *Feral Children and Clever Animals* was particularly useful for me in thinking about these issues. I am especially grateful to my father, Norman Ellis, for many discussions about feral children and their importance to the field of cognitive psychology.

My sister, Emily Ellis, alerted me to the aspects of snail collecting detailed in **The Collectors** and provided me with source material.

Captain Brown's *Book of Butterflies and Moths* is a real book (**Moths**); I was lucky to find a copy in the History of Science Collection at the University of Oklahoma. Much of the information about migraines comes from Oliver Sacks' book *Migraine*.

For information about the "lost twin syndrome," I relied on Peter Whitner's *The Inner Elvis* and various issues of *Weekly World News* (**Twin, Disappearing**). I am grateful to Margaret-Love Denham for suggesting Whitner's book and this poem.

The oddly personal stakes outsiders had (and continue to have) in the case of Anna Anderson, perhaps the most visible of the Anastasia pretenders (**Anna, Anastasia**), is best understood by Peter Kurth's *Anastasia: The Riddle of Anna Anderson*, which was published before DNA testing showed that Anderson was not the daughter of the assassinated Czar Nicholas.

There are a handful of contemporaneous accounts of **The Green Children**, whose identity and origin remains mysterious even if their existence seems certain. William of Newburgh's account appears in *Eyewitness to History*.

Buffalo in Six Directions is for Carter Revard, whose riddle poems inspired the opening and closing of the poem.

The complicated relationships between and among Clara Wieck Schumann (**The Animal Baths**), her husband Franz, and Johannes Brahms have been written about in several biographies, including Nancy Reich's *Clara Schumann: The Artist and the Woman.*

Anna Mae Pictou Aquash (**A Natural History of Hands**) was a Micmac woman and AIM activist murdered on the Pine Ridge Reservation in 1976. Her hands, which were cut off her body by FBI agents, ostensibly for "identification purposes," have been the subject of many poems and have become an essential detail in the history of the American Indian Movement. For a history of AIM and Aquash's life and death, see Peter Matthiessen's *In the Spirit of Crazy Horse* and *Like A Hurricane: The Indian Movement from Alcatrez to Wounded Knee* by Paul Chaat Smith and Robert Warrior.

The Way the World Ends was inspired by the 4th Sutra of Patanjali's *The Sutras.* This poem, along with two others, **Dreaming, the Book** of and **One Day the Girl** were written out of my experiences training as an integral yoga teacher in Bacalar, Mexico. I am grateful to Swami Ramananda with whom I studied the sutras and to my teachers from Yogaville: Michael, Letitia, Prajhapati, and Sarita. To them, and to my twenty-five sister students, I dedicate these poems.

Thanks to Elizabeth Sullivan for the first line of **What She Will Sing to You**.

Acknowledgments

"The Fish Girl" (as "The Lost Mermaid") appeared in the *Atlanta Review*.

"Offices of Pity" in *Nimrod*.

"Sister of the Swans" in *The Poets' Grimm: 20th Century Poems form Grimm Fairy Tales*, ed. Jeanne Marie Beaumont. & Claudia Carlson. Storyline Press, 2003.

"The Moths" in *Many Mountains Moving*, in press.

"What She Will Sing to You" in the *Mid-American Review*.

"The Animal Baths" appeared in *Hika*.

"Anna, Anastasia" in *E: Emily Dickinson Award*, Universities Press West.

"The Green Children" in *Crab Orchard Review*.

"Children of Animals" in *Cimarron Review*.

"Buffalo in Six Directions" in *Sail: Studies in American Indian Literature*.

"Letter from the Crimea" in *Helios*.

"The Orphan Train" in the *Women's Review of Books*.

"A Natural History of Hands" in *Salt*.

"Ghost Ranch" in *TriQuarterly*.

"The Collectors" in *Wild In Our Breast For Centuries: Women and the Returning Realities of War*. Ed. MariJo Moore. Fulcrum Publishing, in press.

"Twin Disappearing," "The Daughter of No One," "Interview with the Reader," "The Collectors," and "Ghazal of Body" appeared in *storySouth*.

For the time and space to work on these poems, I am grateful to The MacDowell Colony, Ragdale, the Ucross Foundation, The Virginia Center for the Creative Arts, Fundacion Valparaiso, Hedgebrook, Norcroft. Special thanks to the Hambidge Center for two extended residencies, which allowed me to finish this book, and for making the world safer for bears, trees, and writers.

Thanks also to the University of Oklahoma and the Robert P Hubbard Fund of Kenyon College for funds that allowed me to travel to these colonies.

The lines from "Meditations for a Savage Child", from DIVING INTO THE WRECK: Poems 1971–1972 by Adrienne Rich. Copyright ©1973 by W. W. Norton & Company, Inc. Used by permission of the author and W. W. Norton & Company, Inc.

Many people have supported the creation of this book. Thanks to Lynn Domina, Joseph Campana, Nancy Johnson, Ishle Yi Park, Ellen Arnold, Chad Allen, Joel Tobin, Jerry Harp, Deborah Miranda, Lesley Wheeler, Allison Hedge Coke; the Norman, Oklahoma writers group, Lara Candland, Julie Gozan, Yun Wang; the Wordcraft Circle; and everyone at SALT, John Kinsella, Chris Hamilton-Emery, Jen Hamilton-Emery.

And all my kin.

Lightning Source UK Ltd.
Milton Keynes UK
UKOW04f0151280415

250471UK00002B/39/P